TRUMP REPUBLICANS ARE DEAD TO ME

David B. McCoy

Spare Change Press ™

Trump Republicans are Dead to Me @ 2021 by
David B. McCoy

ISBN: 978-0-945568-70-4

To:

Mouse

The Lincoln Project

The Bulwark

Carl Bernstein

Spare Change Press TM
Est. 1979
sparechangepress79@gmail.com

NO, I WILL NOT BE 'REACHING OUT' TO
TRUMP VOTERS, NOW OR EVER.
(Title of an Internet article worth reading by
Jamie Davis Smith)

If you know someone who
- Supports and/or follows Trump,
- Believes the election was rigged and Trump won—the "Big Lie",
- Views those who stormed the Capitol on Jan 6, 2021 as patriots,
- Still believes Covid-19 is a hoax and refuses to get a vaccine,
- Believes any of the QAnon conspiracies,
- Views Trump as a god-like figure,
- Continues to fly a Trump Flag,

understand they are part of the TRUMPIAN CULT and NO amount of debating is going to change them. Only by ending your friendship with them might you actually get their attention.

The cover painting:

***

*Delusional cult leaders create delusional
followers.*

Fran Ferder & John Heagle

***

*Donald Trump is our own American war
criminal.*

Carl Bernstein

A villanelle (vil-uh-nell) is a French verse form consisting of five three-line stanzas and a final quatrain, with the first and third lines of the first stanza repeating alternately in the following stanzas. These two refrain lines then form the final couplet in the quatrain.

The villanelle has only two rhymes that repeat throughout the poem. Each of the tercets follows the rhyme scheme ABA, while the quatrain follows the pattern ABAA.

"Though most modernist poets in the 20th century had very little respect for the villanelle (regarding the strictness of its form as stifling to their creativity)," in my writing, I drop one stanza, use both true rhyme and slant (near) rhyme, and use syllabic meter where each line has the same number of syllables (most of the time) but the number of stresses varies.

True rhyme is a form of rhyme that stresses the vowel sound. For example, "sky" and "high" are an example of two words that have a true rhyme

Most slant rhymes are formed by words with identical consonants and different vowels. "Wo**rm**" and "swa**rm**" are examples of slant rhymes.

Note:

Two months after President Joe Biden took office, I drove past a one-time friend's house. When I saw he was flying a Trump flag, I was shocked and directed my ire into writing these poems.

*A reference to Jethro Tull's *Thick As A Brick*

"Thick as a Brick" is a very common saying in England to mock someone's intellect. The first stanza of the first song, explicitly refers to this:

Really don't mind if you sit this one out
My word's but a whisper your deafness a shout
I may make you feel but I can't make you think

#1

Those Trumpians cause me to sigh
Because they are all brainsick;
With no damn shame they freely lie.

Yes, I could punch one in the eye
Just like I would to any dumb hick.
Those Trumpians cause me to sigh.

Every damn one of them tests my
Faith to the point they make me sick.
With no damn shame they freely lie.

I wonder how they can rely
And embrace such nonsense so quick...
Those Trumpians cause me to sigh.

With great comfort I can thereby
Declare them as 'thick as a brick.'*
Those Trumpians cause me to sigh;
With no damn shame they freely lie.

* Government Coordinating Council
** Complete title: National Election Defense
Coalition

#2

—To our very own Trumpian, Rep. Bob Gibbs.

The fact is—there were no rigged elections.
Bill Barr stated there was no voter fraud.
Only screwballs make such dumb assumptions.

Even judges rejected superstitions
that the fall elections were marked with fraud.
The fact is—there were no rigged elections.

After the GCC's* investigation,
They reported no evidence of fraud.
Only screwballs make such dumb assumptions.

National Election Coalition**
Also found no *electronic* fraud.
The fact is—there were no rigged elections.

Therefore, the rational conclusion
Is that to believe in the Big Lie is odd.
The fact is—there were no rigged elections.
Only screwballs make such dumb assumptions.

#3

Why commit germ warfare on their own kind?
The precautions are so very simple.
This would cause poor Darwin to lose his mind.

It's not very hard to ID their kind—
To those *with masks*, they are less than civil.
Why commit germ warfare on their own kind?

"I'm not hurting anyone" is a sign
They're sadly a bunch of mental cripples;
This would cause poor Darwin to lose his mind.

High covid rates in Trump regions remind
Us their numbers will simply dwindle.
Why commit germ warfare on their own kind?

Social distancing also comes to mind
As a good way to avoid the simple.
Why commit germ warfare on their own kind?
This would cause poor Darwin to lose his mind.

*Rep. Elise Stefanik (R-NY), elevation to a Republican Party leadership position—in place of the ousted Rep. Liz Cheney (R-WY)—announced, "We are unified in working with President Trump."

#4

Oh QAnon. Oh QAnon,
Your followers are punch-drunk nuts.
As you know—they're easy to pawn.

You are quite a phenomenon
With members acting like robots.
Oh QAnon. Oh QAnon.

Your "breadcrumbs" require lexicons,
For your meanings have no shortcuts.
And as you know—they're stupid pawns.

Their hunt for pedophiles goes on
But they can't find any hideouts.
Oh QAnon. Oh QAnon.

Now Elise* says she'll carry on
Your grand plan like some mangy mutt.
Oh QAnon. Oh QAnon;
You sure can spot an easy pawn.

* Rep. Bob Gibbs
**Rep. Andrew Clyde

#5

They staged a damn insurrection—
That disgusting gang of traitors!
Worse, it was at Trump's direction.

Fed on lies from politicians—
Even our own legislator* —
They staged a damn insurrection.

Tales of a stolen election
Brought out a mass of rioters.
Worse, it was at Trump's direction.

With bats & polls & collections
Of deadly accelerators,
They staged a damn insurrection—

Tourists?** It was pure aggression!
Scum marched through the Senate chambers.
They staged a damn insurrection.
Worse, it was at Trump's direction.

Everything Trump Touches Dies is the title of a book by Rick Wilson.

#6

The truth is *everything Trump touches dies*.*
Vodka, casinos, airlines, even steaks.
You have to admit he's not very wise.

We should have known that when he turned his
eyes
Toward politics the system would break.
The truth is *everything Trump touches dies*.

Hell, if asked, even I could have advised
Against joining sides with that rattlesnake.
Sadly, so many are not very wise.

And that act he's a populist belies
The fact he views his base as fruitcakes.
They'll soon learn *everything Trump touches
dies*.

But that will not happen until he ties
Those lame-brain republicans to a stake.
You have to admit they're not very wise.
The truth is *everything Trump touches dies*.

* Yobbo: a cruel and brutal fellow
Synonyms: bully, hooligan, roughneck, rowdy, ruffian

#7

The words Trump uses are absurd.
Stupid • Shady • Wacky • Weirdo.
His base swears they're hearing songbirds.

And indeed, they are for his herd—
Nutty • Nasty • Dummy • Dumbo.
The words Trump uses are absurd.

A clown could make this choice of words—
Moonbeam • Moon face • Phony • Psycho.
His base swears they're hearing songbirds.

And each is meant as a smear word—
Leakin' • Loser • Wild Bill • Bozo.
The words Trump uses are absurd.

Of course, there are many you've heard,
But enough about this yobbo.*
The words Trump uses are absurd.
His base swears they're hearing songbirds.

* Here I am referring to Trump Republicans

#8

Republicans* are dead to me.
They believe everything Trump says.
They won't open their eyes to see.

Their brains must be the size of peas
Because that man says some real gems.
Republicans are dead to me.

It's sad to watch them take a knee,
Thinking Trump is some brilliant wiz.
They won't open their eyes to see.

And then there is that spiteful glee
Which always brings me to tears.
Republicans are dead to me.

I'm so glad a few friends agree,
So I won't live in misery.
Republicans are dead to me.
They won't open their eyes to see.

#9

Show your friends you're extremely wise
And admit climate change is real.
Don't fall for another 'Big Lie.'

Scientists have no reason to lie
Or conjure up some bogus spiel.
Show your friends you're extremely wise.

It *does* matter if someone dies
From fumes of an automobile.
Don't fall for another 'Big Lie.'

Thank gawd solar is on the rise;
Compared to fossil fuels it's ideal.
Show your friends you're extremely wise.

Not to act is to jeopardize
All that we believe is ideal.
Don't fall for another 'Big Lie.'
Show your friends you're extremely wise.

* In George Orwell's dystopian 1949 novel *Nineteen Eighty-Four*, the proles are the working class of Oceania. The word prole is a shortened variant of proletarian, which is a Marxist term for a working-class citizen.

#10

There's no hope for you—you're part of the Cult
Of Trump and his deceptive mind control.
To my dying day I will call you out.

So you're unhappy—but it's your own fault
By deciding to remain a prole.*
There's no hope for you—you're part of the cult.

What really flipped you like a somersault
Was the day Obama won at the polls.
To my dying day I will call you out.

You're now a neofascist who exalts
Regaining your perceived loss of control.
There's no hope for you—you're part of the cult.

Through your behavior you mount an assault
On our multiracial, national soul.
To my dying day I will call you out.
There's no hope for you—you're part of the cult.

*Rep. Bob Gibbs aligned himself with Trump's version of reality, even after a House GOP agreement had been struck on the nature of the committee to establish an independent commission to investigate the violent insurrection on Jan. 6 at the US Capitol.

On May 3, Mr. Gibbs released a statement to the House Committee on Oversight and Reform. In that, Mr. Gibbs said, "The lack of transparency and politicians avoiding accountability are major factors why the American people feel so disconnected and ignored by Washington."

If he believes this, why did Gibbs vote NO for an independent commission? The answer is found in the title of the article written by Jennifer Bendery on May 20, "GOP Lies Fueled The Capitol Riot. Of Course They Don't Want A Panel To Expose That."

#11

Those Trump flags say one thing: Traitors!
Like when they charged the Capitol
To anoint Trump their dictator.

Peaceful demonstrators
They were not—more like animals.
Those Trump flags say one thing: Traitors!

They were sure they were crusaders
Charging through a symbolic wall
To anoint Trump as dictator.

They assaulted police officers
In what was plainly a brawl.
Those Trump flags say one thing: Traitors!

Now I hear my legislator*
Claim he never joined the cabal
To anoint Trump as dictator.
Those Trump flags say one thing: Traitors!

#12

I am appalled that your beliefs are based on hate
and unfounded conspiracy theories.
Trump knew all along you would take his bait.

Were those thoughts there all along just wait-
ing till there were no liabilities.
I am appalled that your beliefs are based on hate.

I have to believe the feelings were great
When you could put on those MAGA parties.
Trump knew all along he would take his bait.

Drinking and smoking until it was late,
you talked up Trump's man-made prophecies.
I am appalled that your beliefs are based on hate.

Over time you worked yourself into a state
That when Trump lost you revealed your true
species.
I am appalled that your beliefs are based on hate.
Trump knew all along you would take his bait.

*Shrews have a foul odor caused by scent glands on the flanks as well as other parts of the body.

#13

I believe the Amish are right,
As long as you hold MAGA views
I should keep you out of my sight.

Quite frankly it's pointless to fight
Anyone who holds cultist views.
I believe the Amish are right.

You're no patriot—you're downright
Fascist with that hatred you spew.
I should keep you out of my sight.

The faith of the Amish is forthright—
But yours of Trump looks askew.
I believe the Amish are right.

You might think you're so bloody bright
But you'll be remembered as a shrew.*
I believe the Amish are right,
I should keep you out of my sight.

#14

Face it— You're not pro-American.
Our source of pride you reject out of hand;
You throw our heritage in a trashcan.

You now "support and defend" Trump more than
The Constitution of our great land.
Face it— You're not pro-American.

Now "law and order" Republicans,
After the riot, keep their heads in the sand.
You pitch our heritage in a trashcan.

The once "peaceful transfer of power" can
No longer be counted on with your brand.
Face it— You're not pro-American.

Our "Sweet Land of Liberty' has become an
Arena of carnage by your cruel hands.
Face it— You're not pro-American.
You pitch our heritage in a trashcan.

#15

There is a chilling rise of fascism.
The GOP launched this full-scale war.
Their basis is one of fatalism

With a god ignorant of federalism,
And clearly rotten to the core.
There is a chilling rise of fascism.

Aren't they creating a great schism
By bringing a false idol before God?
Their basis is one of fatalism

Engulfed in their Cult of Satanism.
To state plainly, they're now Donald Trump's
whores.
There is a chilling rise of fascism.

Perhaps an old-fashioned exorcism
Is in order to terminate this fraud.
There is a chilling rise of fascism.
Their basis is one of fatalism.

*Luddites were British weavers and textile workers who objected to the increased use of mechanized looms and knitting frames. Neo-luddites are those who object to the new service-information age (i.e. manufacturing moving out of the U.S.).

#16

Trumpites are a bunch of Neo-luddites.*
Ned Ludd destroyed machines out of protest.
Trumpites engaged in a similar plight.

Trumpites were willing to put up a fight
Against robots who have no need for rest.
Trumpites are a bunch of Neo-luddites.

Strikes once showed the strength of their might,
but it did not take long for them to become pests.
Their encounter was like Ned's failed plight.

Thinking their employment was a birthright
led companies to look elsewhere to invest.
Trumpites are a bunch of Neo-luddites.

This left many with a feeling of blight
Who looked to a charlatan in zest.
Trumpites are a bunch of Neo-luddites.
Trumpites engaged in a similar plight.

* Republican Right

** Second Amendment

Former Chief Justice Warren Burger, a conservative, said the idea that there was an individual right to bear arms was "a fraud." If he were writing the Bill of Rights now, he said in 1991, "There wouldn't be any such thing as the Second Amendment."

"This has been the subject of one of the greatest pieces of fraud, I repeat the word fraud, on the American public by special interest groups that I have ever seen in my lifetime." Former Supreme Court Chief Justice Warren Burger on the Second Amendment, in 1991

#17

The 'Right'* defiles the Second Amendment.
Everything they claim distorts the Founders.
They would never dare change the
                                    Commandments.

It is true its** wording sounds ambivalent,
Yet, the Founders found it clear to their ears.
The "Right" defiles the Second Amendment.

That's because militias were an element
of life to confront British Soldiers.
They would never dare change the
                                    Commandments.

Then weapons were in short supply, which
meant
Each was to provide his own under orders.
The "Right" defiles the Second Amendment.

When the Army became the replacement,
The right to arms went to the government.
The 'Right' defiles the Second Amendment.
They would never dare change the
                                    Commandments.

#18

Trump followers are self-delusional
To a degree never before seen.
For such a modern world, it's just surreal.

The stuff they believe is juvenile—
Like how they'll drop dead from a vaccine.
Trump followers are self-delusional.

And every conversation turns, as usual,
To "Taking our guns" – which to me sounds
pretty keen.
For such a modern world, it's just surreal.

How can they fall for a "disputable
Election?" –the proof can clearly be seen.
Trump followers are self-delusional.

Everything they believe I find despicable,
And I'm **not** sorry if you think I'm mean!
Trump followers are self-delusional.
For such a modern world, it's just surreal.

#19

Trumpites believe every damn thing he says—
Goofy shit like, *I'm a stable genius.*
Can't they step back and just observe what he
does?

Nobody respects women more than me.
Nobody's better to people with disabilities than
me.
Trumpites believe every damn thing he says.

Nobody knows more about nuclear weapons
than me.
Nobody knows more about ISIS than me.
Can't they step back and just observe what he
does?

Nobody knows more about technology than me.
Nobody knows more about renewables than me.
Trumpites believe every damn thing he says.

Nobody knows more about jobs than me.
Nobody builds walls better than me.
Can't they step back and just observe what he
does?

Nobody is more conservative than me.
Nobody loves the Bible more than me.
Trumpites believe every damn thing he says.
Can't they step back and just observe what he
does?

#20

Your degree of treason is off the scale.
What's your goal? To shred the Constitution?
Why should we live with such betrayal?

How you fall for his obvious large-scale
Lies is beyond my comprehension.
Your degree of treason is off the scale.

I would arrest and throw your ass in jail,
Making sure bail would never be an option.
Your degree of treason is off the scale.

If in charge, I would do more to curtail
Your stab at another insurrection.
Why should we live with such betrayal?

Installing Trump may be your Holy Grail
But it's an out-right act of sedition.
Your degree of treason is off the scale.
Why should we live with such betrayal?

#21

For five years I saw you as gullible—
Conned by a professional charlatan,
Then after the count you became trouble.

Shockingly you were unreasonable—
Moving way past just being partisan.
For five years I saw you as gullible.

You were no longer voting for an able
Candidate but an orange-faced harlequin.
Then after the count you became trouble.

And when he lost, you were first to enable
His 'stolen election' –causing a tailspin.
You, by this point, were more than gullible.

Your kind? Sociopaths, with such labels:
Tend to lie, break laws, do anything to win.
For five years I saw you as gullible—
You are nothing but a gang of trouble.

*Dross: The scum or refuse matter which is thrown off, or falls from, metals in smelting the ore, or in the process of melting

**2021: Myanmar (Burma) coup d'état: On February 1, State Counsellor Aung San Suu Kyi and President Win Myint were arrested by the military of Myanmar. The military announced that power had been handed to Min Aung Hlaing, the commander-in-chief of the armed forces. The military announced on state-run TV that they would be in control of the country for one year.

#22

The flag you fly is the new southern cross.
It takes its place next to the Stars & Bars.
It's a display that Trump controls your thoughts.

Nobody sees you as some Betsy Ross,
But instead someone who is quite vulgar.
That flag you fly is the new southern cross.

All of your ideas resemble dross*
And deserve to be thrown hither and far.
Your flag makes clear that Trump controls your
thoughts.

Anti-Semitic slurs are embossed
There with hate and other ways to scar.
The flag you fly is the new southern cross.

While January 6 was a loss,
Your flag says you yearn for a Myanmar. **
The flag you fly is the new southern cross.
It's a display that Trump controls your thoughts.

#23

Trump was not reelected president,
So you embraced the first conspiracy.
But there's no reinstatement precedent.

Fifty judges stated it's self-evident
Trump's cronies have succumbed to tyranny.
Donald Trump is no longer president.

August twelfth is marked as the next big event,
But you know there's no possibility—
There is no reinstatement precedent.

Then what? You're clearly not hesitant
To make voting an impossibility.
Face it, Trump will never be president.

Despite the size of your heart-filled movement,
History will nix your credibility.
Trump was not reelected president,
And there's no reinstatement precedent.

* The act of recalling old information about a subject or a concept like American government or citizenship.

#24

How dare you aid and abet Trump's
Assault on our democracy?
You really need a good brain dump*—

As in, what you were taught, then lumped
in your brain haphazardly.
Is this why you encourage Trump?

You come off like a country bump-
Kin—Autocrats are all ghastly.
You really need a good brain dump.

You'll soon learn how high you can jump
When Trump demands all the booty.
Go ahead, aid and abet Trump—

ALL your rights will go in the dump,
And you'll learn it's no comedy.
How dare you aid and abet Trump?
You really need a good brain dump.

David B. McCoy earned his history teaching degree from Ashland University and his graduate degree from Kent State University. After teaching thirty-two years, David retired to write short books on a wide variety of topics. Before turning to non-fiction, he spent nearly 40 years studying and writing poetry. This collection is his first return to poetry in nearly 10 years.

sparechangepress.weebly.com

amazon.com/author/davidmccoy

TRUMP'S LIES & TWEETS DISTILLED INTO SHORT, CHARMING POEMS

Sold by Amazon.com

How I Discovered Donald Trump is a
Monster

Sold by Amazon.com